7/6/06

Dr. Dortch,
I appreciate you as my
Pastor; and thank you for
your prayers for me this
past week. Jackie Rennick

A Caged Bird's Dream

By

Jackie Rennick

Jackie Rennick

ISBN: 0-9748427-0-2

Designed by
Write-Choice Services, Inc.
P.O. Box 5736, Thomasville, GA 31758
www.write-choiceservices.com

Dedicated to
my children and
the sweet husband of my sunset years,
Tom.

Poetry

Poets are artists,
imaginative and creative with
language.
Their carefully chosen words
capture the mind,
inflame the imagination,
and intoxicate the senses.

Poetry—one of the earliest
expressions of literature—
reveals lifestyles, actions, and
emotions of civilization.

Though narrative and lyric,
Poetry
infuses truth, enhances myth,
esteems heroes, and
inspires love,
keeping reader enthralled
yesterday, today, and forever …

Table of Contents

A Caged Bird's Dream 11
Wind 13
But an Interlude 14
I Made A Rainbow 15
Hibiscus 17
Beautiful Color 18
Think Positive 20
Beauty of the Relationship 21
Gift of Endurance 22
Dream of Equality 23
Clear the Clutter 25
Time of Mind 26
The Salvation Army 27
New Year 28
Steadfast in the Faith 29
Exit to the Future 30
A New Presence 31
Intangible Gold 32
Divine Power 33
A Gift to Behold 34
Just A Carpenter, Mary's Boy? 36
God's Gift 38
Man's Final Choice 39
Looking Down 41
He Is Risen 42
Prayer 46
Healing Balm 48
Expression of Gratitude 49
My Child's Passage 50
Captured Childhood 52

Youth 53
God's Most Precious Gift 54
I Hate the Cold 56
Brief Analogy of Life 57
What If 58
God's Glorious Light 59
The Little Wicker Rocker 60
Never To Be Revisited 62
God's Visual Promise 64
Time 65
All These Things 66
Twice Born 67
Worthy of Praise 68
America Under Attack Prayer 69
A Restless Mind 70
Treasures of the Sea 71
Uninvited Thespians 72
Buoyed By Faith 73
Secure In Orbit 74
Lillian's Birthday (An Essay) 75
Mother's Mirror (An Essay) 77
Mother's Mirror (by Robyn Rennick) 79
Letter From Carolyn 80
Guilt 81
Praises 82
The Real Party Began 83
Mother Is A Woman 85
Uniquely Woman 86
And They Danced 87
Personal Epiphany 88
A Season Continual 89
The Spirit of Praise 90
I Am Satisfied 91
It Takes Courage 92
Cat 93
Life's Sunset 94

Divine Fruit 95
Summertime In Maine 96
Perfect Pitch 97
Proverb 98
The Son of God 99
Quick Fix 100
Hurricane 101
Birthday Surprise 102
Focused 103
Cultivate 104
Life's Finished Tapestry 105
Invisible Dove 106
Never to Be Contained 107
Environmental Graveyard 108
Blaze A Trail 109
For A Moment 110
Presence of the Moment 111
The Open Door 112
Eternal Fellowship 113
A Red Traffic Light 114
Twilight 115
Hawaiian Paradise 116
Messenger Of Grace 118
The Star 119
Unafraid 120
Paula's Spirit 121
PAN 123
Sweetening the Filling 124
Family Reunion 125
Cancer 126
Birthdays 127
Birthday—Again 128
Glory of Christmas 129
Promise of Peace 130
Prayer Is the Formula 131

About the Author 133

A Caged Bird's Dream

I have never seen the world
Except through bars.
It is out there, beyond the bars,
All the beauty of it:
Trees, flowers, sunshine, and
Other birds just like me.

Day after day, month after month,
I sit in this cage—
A mere spectator of life passing
Beyond my bars.

I sometimes sing, but for what reason
I'm not quite sure;
An inherent gene, I suppose.
And it pleases my lady.

She is good to me:
Provides for me, cleans my cage, and
Sometimes talks to me;
But she never allows me freedom.
When she hangs my cage on the porch,
This prison becomes more confining.
For out there, beyond my bars,
I see a world of awesome wonder;
Birds flying free through the green trees
Calling joyfully to their mates.

Oh, to escape this prison!
To soar
Into the limitless, blue, blue sky,
To feel
The warmth of sunshine on my feathers;
Air currents beneath my wings.
A caged bird's dream. ...

Wind

I hear it approach,
Feel its presence.
Although I can't see it,
There is a freshness of air,
A rustle of the green
Coolness on my face …
A waiting expectancy.

The katydids feel it—
Stop their incessant noise.
With outstretched arms,
Upturned face,
I wait expectantly.
All is quiet—
The wind has died.

But An Interlude

Frozen into a brittle, brown sculpture by
Seasonal cold,
The barren landscape procrastinated,
Awaited moderation—
The warm fingers of the sun to unlock
The miracle of spring.
Then winter would be remembered as
But an interlude—
A necessity of rest and regeneration
From which would rise
The glorious ... awesome ... spring.

I Made A Rainbow

I made a rainbow today!
I know:
You will say, "That is silly, for
Only God can make a rainbow."
But really I did. I made a rainbow!

Today wasn't my best day.
It was one of those days when
Nothing seems to go well.
My head ached, the children were cross, and
My husband complained that he had no clean socks.

It was a day when one wonders,
Why did I get out of bed!
I was beginning to think that
Life had become a boring drudge.

To escape self-pity,
I went outside to water the plants.
I didn't notice that the sun was shining brightly
Until I turned on the hose and
Arched a stream of water into the air.
That was when I saw it!
A rainbow of glorious, shimmering colors,
Trapped in the water and sunshine.

I was so excited,
I forgot my headache, as well as
The cares of the morning.
Laughing like a happy child,
I thanked God for his provision of grace,
Allowing me to make a rainbow.

"I do sit my rainbow in the cloud,
And it shall be a covenant between
Me and the earth." —*Genesis 9:13*

Hibiscus

Have you seen the hibiscus bloom?
I have!
Kissed by the morning sun,
The tightly furled buds,
Showing a border of vibrant color,
Puff importantly ...
But they don't open immediately,
For the rising of the sun governs their
Blooming.

The sun begins its heavenly ascent;
The buds relax.
The petals slowly begin to unfurl—
The crimson-colored, trumpet-shaped flowers
Exposing slender pistils,
Crowned with delicate gold and crimson stamen;
God's creative work of art.

The life of the hibiscus bloom is brief—
Rising sun to setting sun.
But I enjoy this transient beauty
(So do the ants and hummingbirds).
Its exotic flowers dominate my garden.

Beautiful Color

Why can't they see beyond the
Color of my face?
Why can't they see that I'm no different than they?
I see … I hear,
I laugh … I cry,
I walk … I talk …
And I dream significant dreams:

I wish to live in a land of total freedom,
In a house with a garden
Filled with flowers of all colors—
Not segregated in beds of one color,
But a mass array of gloriously combined colors.

And when I go shopping,
I don't want to be covertly watched,
Mentally catalogued as a shoplifting risk.
I want to be greeted pleasantly as a welcome customer,
Courted as a future client.

I want to feel secure and comfortable
Anywhere in the bus—
Enjoy freedom in its entirety as
My rightful heritage;
Know that if I prepare myself,
I am capable of becoming whatever
I desire to be.

When I apply for college,
I don't want to be one of a quota.
I want to be a person in my own right—
One who is accepted to grow intellectually,
That I may go forth from that place and utilize
The knowledge I have acquired.

As a single vote:
I want my life to count—
Count for myself and for all mankind,
That the world will no longer be divided but
Unified.

My face:
A flower of beautiful, harmonious color
Enhancing the garden of life.

Think Positive

I am disillusioned—disturbed.
Former achievements are meaningless,
For the joy of living has departed.
I'm the casualty of an accident not of
My making.

The shadow of day lengthens into
Long, restless night.
I dwell in the darkness of netherland,
Captive to anxiety and fear.

I am unable to control my thoughts.
Then my Soul speaks,
Reminding me:
"God is aware of each sparrow that falls;
He is also aware of your needs."

I want to believe—I pray
For an infusion of His healing love.
Timidly, I dare to believe that
"This, too, shall pass."

Raising my head wearily,
I can see the dawning of a new day.
Faith renewed,
I begin to think positive.

Beauty of the Relationship

Deep in my angry heart a tremor
Grows in intensity, until
I am shaken from my passion of rage,
Forced to look beyond self ... and to my surprise,
A hummingbird appears!

Not the common, garden-variety
Hummingbird,
But a *miraculous* hummingbird!
Its feathers jeweled iridescence,
A gold, elongated beak,
And Brilliant turquoise eyes
In which the clarity of fear is vanquished.

My anger is suddenly replaced
By inconceivable joy!
Like a child, I laugh out loud
At the maneuvers of this miraculous bird.
Soaring, dipping, darting, hovering,
It savors the delicious nectar,
Careful not to damage the beauty of the flower.

Its desire satisfied,
The hummingbird is gone—as is my anger.
I smile,
Deciding that in the future, I shall
Savor life's nectar more appreciatively,
Be careful not to damage
The beauty of the relationship.

Gift of Endurance

The world refers to us as
Super Women—
Or is it just the men who so quip?
But it's true!

Mothers continually walk the
High wire,
While carrying the progeny of life
On their slim shoulders.

Afraid to look down;
They look up—giving thanks to God
For His unique gift of endurance ...
Mother's love.

Dream of Equality

Being a woman isn't easy.
Being a woman is …
Being what others think that
A woman should be.

A woman is programmed from
Birth until death;
First by Mother, whose desire is to
Make her a replica of self.

Then by teachers of primeval opinion,
"Women don't have the mental capacity of
Men,"
And try to funnel them into
Feminine careers.

In marriage:
Woman is expected to work a full-time job,
Bear and nurture children,
Keep the house,
Be a playmate to her husband.

In retirement:
A woman doesn't dare appear
Old and weary.
She is expected to remain attractive—
Trim and fit,
With an energy level surpassing his.

In death:
Woman is made-up to conceal the
Ravages of her weariness.
While she lies in rest—
In transition between physical and spiritual—
Does woman dream of equality?

Clear the Clutter

Talk, talk, talk ...
And rarely do I listen to myself—
Hearing my own voice makes me very
Nervous.

When I do listen,
I wonder if I'm repeating myself.
The words are so familiar ...
It seems I've heard them ofttimes before.

It is my short-term memory—
I think that I have completely lost it!
I can't remember today what
I said yesterday.

It is said, "Repeating one's words is
A sure sign of growing old."
I'm not convinced.
It could be the brain discarding verbiage.

Suffering overload, the brain has
Short-circuited
And doesn't respond to word command.
Repeats, repeats, repeats ...

Perhaps the brain only needs
Restorative therapy:
"Practice, think before speaking ... and listen."
Reprogrammed, I now remember.

Time of Mind

Going backward in time of mind,
I was amazed at the lucidity of
Remembrance.
Thoughts long obscured in the tunnel of
Forgetfulness,
Now highlighted in the clarity of focus.
The most intimate of moments
Were reviewed,
Creating their own season of satisfaction.
Exciting a void of lonely emptiness to
Stellar explosion!

Going backward in time of mind—
Propelled forward into the excitement of living.

The Salvation Army

"General" William Booth in 1865—
An Englishman with a dream that came alive:
To build an organization of military sight,
Becoming an army of righteous might!

Starting in a ripple by the sea,
Booth never imagined the power it would be,
As it gathered energy from shore to shore,
To become a tidal wave at Heaven's door.

The Salvation Army cares for them all—
The homeless, the sick, the weak, the small;
Never noticing color, creed or race,
But ministering to all ... any time ... any place.

So if you have anything to spare,
This is an organization with which to share.
If it's only two fish and a loaf of bread,
Through God's love and grace,
A multitude will be fed.

New Year

Thank you, Father, for this
New Year.
Thank you for the privilege of life,
The opportunity to share new experiences,
To enjoy the constant excitement of
Your ever-changing world.

What a privilege it is to be
A citizen of
The United States of America!
Let us not forget that citizenship is not
To be taken lightly, but with it comes
Great responsibility. …

So we pray for guidance,
For ourselves as individuals, and
Collectively,
That our beloved country may continue
To develop as a land of opportunity and
Freedom
For all people who seek a better way of life.

Let us never forget that
A country's strength comes from within,
That our nation's growth is
Nurtured
IN GOD WE TRUST.

Steadfast in the Faith

A new millennium—many predictions,
Some that may become reality,
As did the birth of God's Son, Jesus,
Proclaimed by angels two thousand years ago.

In acknowledgement of Jesus' birth,
We celebrate Christmas and
The New Millennium,
Believing all prophecy will be fulfilled.
Until that time,
We remain steadfast in the faith.

Exit to the Future

While past experiences can become
Shadows on the present,
The shadows need not become the
Determining factor for future failure, unless
We (as Lot's wife) choose
To look backward, becoming pillars of salt.

Molded into this position,
Forever looking over our shoulder,
We are trapped in a time warp of our making.
Preoccupied with the past,
The present becomes a dark tunnel ...
Without exit.

But escape is possible!
We must ask God for foresight ... and
Spiritual strength to leave the past behind.
Now committed to moving forward,
We find exit to the future.

A New Presence

I stand motionless in the shade,
Afraid to move into the sunshine—
Afraid I might see my shadow.
Shadow is something I don't acknowledge;
It scares me!

For to cast a shadow is evidence of
A physical being;
Somewhere in my body of emptiness
A real person does exist!

But who is this living presence
I'm afraid to feel?
I might freak out if I discover who really
Inhabits my body.

I move out of the shade
(not enough to create shadow),
Feel the warmth of the filtered sun,
Pray that the cold core inside will dissolve
And fill my emptiness.

I raise both arms to the sky,
Twirl and twirl and twirl, until exhausted
I fall to my knees and imploringly
Gaze heavenward.
The dam breaks and tears flow.

Miraculously,
I am cleansed by the flood;
Shadow is washed away.
The warmth of Sonshine fills me with
A new presence.
I give thanks and praise God!

Intangible Gold

How often we seek love,
Only to be denied fulfillment, because
Love isn't an acquisition—
Love is an inward growth process
Manifested in continual, outward action,
Satisfying and nurturing to those involved,
Producing priceless treasure of intangible gold.

Be humble and gentle. Be patient with each other,
Making allowances for each other's faults
Because of your love. (Ephesians 4:2)

Divine Power

Forgive me, God,
For becoming locked into my own
Conception of time and space.
I am alone in here—suffocating!
Experiencing the Hell of claustrophobia.

Incarcerating my mind,
I have also imprisoned my soul.
I am frightened—frightened that
My perception of God has become distorted;
I have recreated You in my image.

Deliver me of this perception.
Remove the shackles from my soul.
Direct my attention upward and outward
To Your spiritual realm,
Which can never be contained
But is continually expanding to reveal
God's divine power.

A Gift To Behold

In the presence of the Shepherd
Life is secure indeed,
For the presence of the Shepherd
Provides our every need.

He is always available, wears
A welcoming smile.
His dear face alight with love,
He beckons his lost child.

Forgotten is yesterday's trial,
When the child ran away.
His forgiveness and loving compassion
Are renewed each and every day.

Waiting by the sheepfold,
A shaft of pure and glorious light,
He holds the gate wide open,
Offering security from the fears of night.

For too much of our life is
Lived in darkness,
With fear covering us like a shroud—
When our only hope is JESUS,
We call His name out loud!

He hears our cry of terror, recognizes
His lost sheep,
Reaching with the staff,
He guides us into the safety of
His keep.

And in the light of His presence,
In the protection of His fold,
The saving grace of Jesus
Is a gift to behold!

Just A Carpenter, Mary's Boy?

"**H**e is just a carpenter, Mary's boy,"
The people sneered.
Oh, but what a carpenter!
Master of His trade.

Jesus
Built inward ... outward ... upward,
Uniquely
Restoring lives to healthy, spiritual quality.

Just a carpenter, Mary's boy?
He forgave sins, healed the sick,
Opened the eyes of the blind,
Cleansed the lepers, and raised the dead!

"He is just a carpenter, Mary's boy."
His hometown couldn't see beyond his
Earthly chronology;
He could do no great miracles there.

Just a carpenter, Mary's boy?
He was born by immaculate conception,
Welcomed by angelic chorus,
Worshipped by Wise Men.

Just a carpenter, Mary's boy?
He was the incarnation of perfect love;
Dying for the sins of humanity.
On the third day, He rose from the dead!

Just a carpenter, Mary's boy:
Yes—
But He was also God's Son—The Messiah!
The promised Saviour of the world.

Know that this is indeed the Christ,
The Saviour of the world. (John 4:42)

God's Gift

In the innocence of the Baby Jesus is seen
The glory of God.
In the intelligence and wisdom of His youth,
God is manifest.
In the walk of His manhood,
God's compassion and grace is evident.
In Jesus' submission to God's will,
Death on the cross at Calvary,
God's love is complete.
In His resurrection—to all who believe—
God's gift is eternal life.

Man's Final Choice

"On the sixth day
God created man in his own image,
In the image of God created he him;
Male and female created he them." *—Genesis 1:27*

Created in God's own image,
Man was given choice.
He chose to ignore the sovereignty of God,
To follow his own rebellious mind.

Fellowship with God severed,
Man was expelled from the Garden of Eden.
Conceived in glory,
Mankind was destined to darkness.

Spiritual apostasy was practiced throughout
The annals of time.
Building his empires on shifting sand,
Mankind ignored divine order

Until
God's grace was revealed
Through the birth of His beloved son,
Jesus Christ,
Who became the Holy Sacrifice for man's sin.

Crucified on the cross at Calvary
And buried in a tomb,
Jesus was resurrected on the third day.
He ascended to Heaven.

Jesus' victory over sin and death
Restored fellowship between God and man.
The fear of eternal death
Replaced by the promise of eternal life.

Man's final choice:
"Believe on the Lord Jesus Christ, and thou shalt be saved."

Looking Down

Looking down from twenty-nine thousand feet,
Through the window of a commercial jet,
The earth below appears a flat plane of variegated greens,
Buildings multicolored chips,
Humans not seen.
I wonder how God, somewhere out there,
Is even aware that we exist.
Then, I gaze upward ... outward,
See the blue expanse of sky without horizon,
But I do not feel isolated—
I feel God inside me,
The loving Spirit that always keeps me tuned to
His presence.
And although I'm only one
In a universe that teems with trillions of souls,
I am unique—God's child—
And He knows me personally.
I am secure.

He Is Risen

The elements were restless—angry.
Gusting winds sent brooding black clouds
Scurrying across the metallic sky—
A storm in the making.

The twisting narrow streets of Jerusalem
Were crowded with pilgrims;
It was Passover;
They had come to worship in the Temple.

But something was amiss.
Beneath the mask of reverence ran a
Current of excitement—
Today there was to be a Roman crucifixion!

The sound of Roman sandals
On cobblestone ... shouts and curses!
Pilgrims roughly shoved aside, clearing a path
For the three condemned men headed to Golgotha.

Two of the men carried their crosses.
A conscripted pilgrim carried the cross of the third.
Bruised and bloody, he wore a crown of platted thorns
And was supported between two Roman soldiers.

Appearing on the verge of collapse,
The man's demeanor was majestic—serene.
On his passing,
The jeering taunts of the crowd were silenced.

For many remembered Jesus, who
Healed the sick, restored the blind, raised the dead;
His only offense being—

He claimed to be the Son of God.

Jealous of his popularity and
Supernatural powers,
The Jewish priests schemed to kill Jesus.
But Pilate found no just cause to crucify him.

But because of political pressure, Pilate relented,
Gave Jesus over to be crucified.
The priests, fearing a riot, nervously scanned
The crowd for troublemakers.

A small group of women
(one pointed out as the mother of Jesus)
Were scornfully taunted, as they sorrowfully
Followed the condemned up the hill of Golgotha.

Lightning flashed and thunder rolled;
And an eerie twilight descended upon the land.
Yelling obscenities, the Roman soldiers hurried to
Complete their gruesome task.

Hanging on the cross
Between brooding sky and shrouded earth,
One of the criminals demanded of Jesus,
"If you are the Messiah, save yourself and save us."
But the other criminal rebuked him. ...

Repenting his sins, he asked to be
Remembered when Jesus came into his kingdom.
Jesus replied,
"This day you shall be with me in Paradise."

The earth shuddered and violently convulsed.
Jesus cried out,
"My God, my God, why have you forsaken me?"
He then dismissed his spirit;
The curtain in the Temple was rent.

Jesus' dead body was given to
Joseph of Arimathea,
Who wrapped it in a linen cloth and placed
It in a new sepulcher hewn in stone.

The priests went to Pilate, asked that
The sepulcher be sealed and guarded,
For Jesus had said,
"After three days I will rise again."

In the early morning of the third day,
The women went to the tomb.
An angel of the Lord met them, saying,
"Why are you looking among the dead for
One who is alive? He is risen!"

Jesus first appeared to the women,
Then appeared to two of his followers at Emmaus.
Returning quickly to Jerusalem,
They found the disciples, who exclaimed,
"The Lord is risen! He has appeared to Simon!"

Suddenly, Jesus was among them, saying,
"Peace be with you."
Seeing his pierced hands and feet,
They reverently touched his physical body, then
Worshipped Him.

Jesus appears again to his disciples in Galilee
And commands them to go to all people, making them
His disciples and baptizing them in the name of
The Father, the Son, and the Holy Spirit,
Teaching them to obey His commandments.
He promises to be with them until the end of the age.

Jesus charged his disciples to remain in
Jerusalem until imbued with the Holy Spirit.
He then led them to Bethany,
Lifted His hands and blessed them.
He was then parted from them and taken up into Heaven.

"Thou are the Christ, the Son of the living God."
—*Matthew 16:16*

Prayer

Lord,
You have walked a long way with me.
The road has been torturous, and
Around every curve lurked danger, but
You were always there,
Holding my hand, leading me,
Speaking soft words of encouragement
In my ear.

Thinking
I was too tired to continue on,
My head drooped;
For my depression was burdensome.
I saw nothing but the weary road ahead;
But you never allowed me to stop,
Whispered,
"Don't lookdown—look up!"

How fortunate that I listened—
Allowed You to guide me.
For You have provided far beyond
My greatest dreams and expectations.
I am in awe of Your never-failing love and
Power ...

A Spiritual force
Emanating from the center of the Universe,
Traveling faster than the speed of light,
Ministering
To a lost child with loving compassion ...
That I might find peace.

I now feel secure in my world because
I have glimpsed your world.
Thank you,
My Savior and my God. Amen.

Healing Balm

When we are forever apart, and there are
Only memories to bridge the gulf between us, to
Relieve the pain of my hurting heart,
I recall Jesus' promise:
"I am the resurrection and the life:
He that believeth in me, though he were dead,
Yet shall he live:
And whosoever liveth and believeth in me
Shall never die."
I believe, and it becomes a
Healing balm to my sorrowful heart.
My pain subsides.
I can now accept that my loved one,
Absent from me in body,
Is now in the presence of God.
My faith restored,
I am able to walk onward,
Confident.
At the end of life's journey
My loved one is waiting, and I shall
Never again be alone.

Expression of Gratitude

Thank you, Jesus, for
Coming to Earth to experience
The problems of mortal life.
Thank you for caring enough that
You chose to sacrifice your
Physical life
In payment for our frailties,
That we might have spiritual life
Everlasting.

"Thanks be to God, which giveth us the victory
Through our Lord Jesus Christ." *—1 Corinthians 15:57*

My Child's Passage

I sat by her bed for days ...
Watching, waiting and praying for change;
But change was always for the worse.
Her body wasted before my eyes.

I ministered with all the love that
A mother is capable of.
Too weak to speak ... she smiled her special smile.
My heart convulsed with her pain, and
My eyes burned with tears that
I dared not shed.

She was much too young to die!
Life was full of dreams to become realities;
But for her ... never to be.
My beloved child was leaving me.
I could not keep her!

Day receded ...
Darkness obliterating evening shadows.
I knew—in my heart I knew—
Night would be the pallbearer for death!
When the sun rose, my child
Would have returned to that from whence
She came. ...

Except for her painful, labored breathing,
The bedroom was quiet.
I bowed my head in humble submission and
Prayed:
"Enough, God, my child has suffered enough.
I can now let her go."

My pain was far more intense
Than when I gave birth.
I rested my throbbing head on her pillow.
I felt a loving touch—a light pat.
Taking her fragile hand, I kissed it gently.
She weakly squeezed my hand and then released it.

Heartbroken:
Perhaps I dozed, perhaps I dreamed, perhaps
God gave me a vision. ...
The ceiling silently opened to a vaulted evening sky
Awash with silvery moonlight and luminous stars.
Then I heard the music—
The most glorious, celestial music!

Eager to share this impromptu heavenly concert
I reached for my child's hand;
It was limp and cold—my child was dead!
I screamed in anguish—the music reached crescendo,
And the ceiling closed. ... I was alone!

My heart was broken,
Yet I was miraculously comforted, for
God had momentarily opened the doors to heaven
To reveal my child's passage.
She was now safe with Him.

Captured Childhood

My children are here—
Happy faces smiling at me through
Frames of glass and gold,
Their pictures evidence of the fruitful season
In my life ... which has almost been.

In this innocent state of captured childhood
They serenely stare back at me,
Unaware of the change that time has wrought.
Forever locked
In their childish memory is the image of
A youthful, smiling mother—arms outstretched ...

And it shall ever be.
For when I'm alone, as I am much these days,
I will make excuses to dust—escaping,
Temporarily, through the gold and glass frames to that
Former life, dispelling my loneliness.

Youth

Like the first dawn,
Youth breaks on the horizon,
Fearing neither terrain in shadow, nor
Pitfall obscure.

Youth is unconcerned that fair dawn
Is deceptive;
Behind its façade of untroubled sky
Lurk storms of violent nature.

Youth is energetic and ambitious:
Knowledge is the key.
Success is the motivation.
Life is the vehicle. Accelerate!

In his incessant busyness,
Youth is lost in birthdays that have been.
Evening shadow foretells day's end.
Alarmed, he cries, "Not yet!
The road is filled with dreams to be achieved!"

Overwhelmed by the avalanche of spent years,
Youth is victim to the caution of maturity.
His thirst for adventure is slaked.
His hectic lifestyle is calmed.

Dreams are less vivid, reality more focused.
Youth is lost in the tuns ...
And as vintage wine in full bouquet is sweet,
Middle age has now become.

God's Most Precious Gift

With the exception of one bright star,
The sky was dark.
Shepherds keeping watch over their flocks
Saw the night sky open, heard
An angel proclaim the birth of the Savior,
Christ the Lord!

There appeared a multitude of heavenly host
Praising God, and saying,
"Glory to God in the highest, and on earth
Peace, good will toward men."
The heavens then closed.

His face aglow, a young shepherd said,
"Let us go to Bethlehem.
Let us see for ourselves this wonderful thing
That has surely come to pass!"

Another shepherd shook his head.
"It was but a dream. ..."
There was much excited discussion.
The majority believed it was God's revelation.

The unbeliever scoffed, "Go, if you must,
But as for me,
I shall stay here and keep watch
Over the sheep!"
Refusing to believe—to follow the star—
He forfeited God's most precious gift.

Those shepherds who chose to believe—
To follow the star—
Found the source of everlasting light—
Baby Jesus, the Son of God.

I Hate the Cold

It is cold outside, and
I hate the cold!
Losing my vim and vitality,
As well as my usual cheerfulness,
I am a bear in hibernation awaiting spring.

The plans
I made for cooler weather went with
The summer's heat.
I don't want to do anything but
Snuggle under a blanket and read a book.

The only thing "hot-wired" around here
Is my ravenous appetite.
Hunger is constant ... to be appeased
At the cost of two dress sizes.

Unlike the bear who comes out of
Hibernation thinner,
In the spring I shall emerge obese ...
A large bearskin substituting for
My summer bikini.

Brief Analogy of Life

A trip to the beach might be
A brief analogy of life:

Walking the beach, I become so
Involved in picking up shells,
I pay no attention to the provider, the ocean.
Becoming so excited upon finding a sand dollar,
I don't notice the beauty of the morning.
Drowned in the music of a boom box,
I am deaf to the songs of sea birds.

Forgetting to lather my body in suntan oil,
I lie down on my blanket,
Think about tomorrow's busy schedule.
Exhausted by the thought, I sleep … to awaken
Sunburned.
Grumpily reviewing my day,
I decide the trip wasn't worth the effort.

What If . . .

What is it about a rainy day
That makes me so introspective, melancholy,
Reverse the hourglass to
Time long past?

But I persist;
And as the radio plays accompaniment for
Raindrops drumming on the skylight,
Memories packed away years ago
Return, bag and baggage,
To litter my mind.

While many of the episodes are
No longer important, they are disquieting;
And each thought must be
Meticulously examined, as I ask myself,
For the zillionth time,
"Did I make the right decision?
What if ..."

God's Glorious Light

Awakening depressed and blue,
I hardly knew what to do.
Then I heard a voice so small
I could hardly hear it at all.
But it refused to be stilled, whispering,
"Why spoil the day?
Why conjure up thoughts of things to go wrong?
Why spoil the day by stilling the song?
Let your spirit soar—allow joy to glow,
Shedding light for those who may not know
Each new day is a gift that God has blessed,
Not a burden of which to be depressed.
Walk with Him for a while—
Your depression will be replaced with a smile.
Your day will become sunshine bright, reflecting
God's glorious light."

The Little Wicker Rocker

There was a little wicker rocker
That sat at the foot of my bed.
I never knew from whence it came, but,
"It's mine!" I always said.

All through my childhood,
When things didn't go just right,
I'd sit in my little wicker rocker and
Its arms would hold me tight.

Back and forth, back and forth I rocked,
Sharing that which I dared not speak,
Knowing the little wicker rocker
Would all my secrets keep.

I continued to grow in stature,
While the little rocker remained the same.
But I refused to notice … and
Still I came.

I sat on the floor
In front of the little chair,
And where I once sat and rocked,
My head now rested there.

Although I didn't rock anymore,
The little chair was aware;
And the comfort of its company
Soothed my every care.

The years rocked by,
And too soon I left home;
But the memory of the little wicker rocker
Forever remains my comfort zone.

Never To Be Revisited

I went on pilgrimage to a
Far place
That I thought was forever forgotten—
Never to be revisited—
And I fought returning there.

For it was a wretched place of
Hurt and loneliness—
A period in my early life that
I wanted to forget.

I had buried the memories
Deep inside,
Covered them with the busyness of living;
But they refused to die,
Making their presence known through
Depression.

Suffering the horrors of depression,
I prayed for the hurts to heal,
To release me
From the anguish I suffered …
But release did not come quickly.

It took years of growth—
Physical, mental and, most important,
Spiritual—
Before God could prepare me to
Face self.

Grief had to be acknowledged,
Unhappy memories forgiven, and anger released.
Only then did
My inward rage and turmoil subside.

Born anew:
I was spiritually and mentally healed by
God's compassionate love.
I am now at peace.

He maketh me to lie down in green pastures.
He leadeth me beside the still waters.
He restoreth my soul. (Psalms 23:2-3)

God's Visual Promise

Last month:
Beyond my kitchen window it was winter and
Nature slept.
The trees were bare and motionless in
The cold of March.

This month ... a dramatic change!
April's warm sunshine
Stimulated the rising of sap, awakening nature.
The landscape now wears
The new, bright seasonal dress of spring.

Returning with spring,
The birds fly through the green-leafed trees,
Inspecting the curvature of limbs, staking
Their summer homestead.

Spring:
Earth is awakened to the newness of
Life.
God's visual promise to us, his children:
Those who sleep in Christ shall be awakened
To the eternal newness of Spiritual life.

Time

Time—
The essence by which life is measured—
Is
The thief that steals precious moments that
Can never be reclaimed.
Fleeing onward is its own light of passage.

Time—
Neither hurried nor slowed—
Punctually devours self.

All These Things

All these things. ... We have prayed,
Oh God,
Forgetting from one prayer to
The next what we ask.
For the pressure of life is so great, and the
Needs so prevalent, that
We become saturated with the
Contents of our prayers, repeating our petitions
Over and over.
But we know that you understand.
You hear and strengthen us,
Encouraging us to believe.
For it is written in Your Word,
"Be not afraid, only believe."
I believe!

Twice Born

Fireflies and butterflies,
Black-eyed Susan fill the ditch;
Green fields, woods with whippoorwills,
Churring loudly in nasal pitch.

Furry kittens and playful puppies
Teaching us to love;
Moonlight and stars bright,
Illuminating the heavens above,

The world is filled with miracles—
All created by God;
But the miracle of greatest worth was
Man created from earth.

Unfortunately,
There were tares in the dirt. ... And
God's most unique creation
Chose a life of sin and degradation.

Eons passed and civilization grew;
However, man's nature remained askew
Until Jesus came.
His mission—man to reclaim.

Through His loving grace and sacrifice,
Man was born not once ... but twice!
Naturally born, he was destined to die.
Spiritually reborn, he would live eternally.

Worthy of Praise

Sometimes we cannot accept praise,
Although the work is superior and
Worthy of praise—inside,
Something continues to deny its value.

When complimented, we are embarrassed,
Often assuming a false attitude,
Saying, "Oh, it is nothing," while
Inside we are yelling, "It is terrific!
I almost 'killed myself' completing this project!"

Why can't we just relax and
Bask in the glow of the accomplishment,
Thank God for the talent, and
Praise one's self for tenacity and perseverance?

Being talented is truly a God-given blessing.
But developing that talent takes
Effort and strong, personal commitment.
That is worthy of praise.

I can do all things through Christ who strengthens me.
(Philippians 4:13)

America Under Attack Prayer

Dear Father and Holy God,
We are torn with grief—
Grief for those who have lost loved ones in
These senseless acts of terror against our nation.
We ask your compassion,
That your divine grace will comfort their hurting hearts.
We pray for America under attack,
That its Spirit will never be diminished by terrorists;
That our faith in your universal power will ever increase;
That you will give us the determination and strength
To protect and preserve our nation.
We ask wisdom and guidance for the President,
And for those who make vital decisions. ...
GOD SAVE AMERICA!

A Restless Mind

A restless mind is not unlike
A restless sea,
With whitecaps frolicking across the
Sparkling water
Toward the beckoning horizon,
Oblivious that the energetic
Force creating this momentum can also
Become movement out of control—
Power deceptive,
Exciting one to forget the
Presence of dangerous undertow,
Capriciously racing toward the open sea.

Treasures of the Sea

"Shells, shells, shells,
A thousand shells ... no, a million shells!"
Katie sang,
As she stooped and scooped and deposited
Shells
In the plastic bag that she carried.

Her big brother, Charlie,
Selecting a Snakeskin Turban for his collection,
Shook his head saying,
"Those are pelecypoda—common scallop shells."
Undaunted,
The five-year-old continued to fill her bag.

"Look at this one."
Katie extended her small hand, palm up.
"Isn't it the coolest?"
"Swollen olive," Charlie said importantly.
Her squeals of delight
Continuing the length of the beach,
She filled her bag and pockets with the
Treasures of the sea.

Uninvited Thespians

I wish the night was more friendly.
Its shadows harbor so many dramatic scenes,
Reminding me of sorrows past.

Illumined by my imaginative memory,
These uninvited thespians
Reenact vivid scenes of painful trauma ...
Better forgotten.

Desperate to escape,
I bury my face in the pillow, and,
Pulling the cover over my head, fervently
Pray for the finale—sleep. ...

Buoyed By Faith

Life is a sea of wild waves driven by
Tornado-strength winds against
Jagged rock cliffs;
Terrified,
I cry out, "Save me, Lord!"

Jesus is ever near.
Hearing my cry, he turns me around,
Directing my attention
Toward the calm waters of the bay.
Buoyed by faith,
I swim against the turbulence.

The swimming is difficult.
The waves pound me and wash over my face,
My muscles ache and I gasp for breath!
But faith keeps me flailing and kicking, as
I swim desperately toward the
Calm waters of the bay.

Finally:
Battered and exhausted, I emerge from the sea.
Coming up and out of the turbulence,
I fall wearily upon the white, sandy beach.
Raising salt-burned eyes heavenward,
I thank God for his saving grace.

Then they cry unto the Lord in their trouble,
And he saves them out of their distresses. (Psalms 107:19)

Secure In Orbit

Katie, my small granddaughter, asked,
"Does the earth move?"
"Yes," I replied, "it orbits around the sun."
After serious thought I recognized
Two great truths:
The earth does revolve around the sun
From which it gets light; but,
The earth also revolves around the Son of God
Who is the Light of the World.
If we walk in His light,
Spiritual gravitation
Will keep us secure—in eternal orbit.

Lillian's Birthday
(An Essay)

God created seraphim, cherubim and angels—created he them in his image of perfection to serve him. Then God created man in his own image to fellowship with him. However, God made mortal man different, allowing him choice, to choose whom he would serve. God's experiment was not totally successful.

Then on November 14th of a blessed year, God sent forth a baby girl to live her mortal life on planet Earth. From the very beginning she was a most unusual child, for God had made her special. He had carefully installed in her the fruits of his Holy Spirit: love, joy, peace, patience, kindness, goodness, faithfulness, gentleness and self-control.

Through her formative years, the child was carefully nurtured in the faith; and she was taught to practice her gifts of grace. Upon becoming a woman, she went forth as a teacher, determined to make a difference in the lives of those she taught. While teaching children the three R's, she never hesitated to plant spiritual seed through example and spiritual truth from the Bible.

As a devoted wife and loving mother, she built her house upon a foundation of faith in Jesus Christ; and the calamities of life were incapable of destroying it.

As a missionary, she became God's Ambassador to the hurting world. Sharing God's message of love and compassion, she breached barriers; and many lost souls were encouraged to repent and find their peace in serving our Lord.

Her goal is literacy for the masses ... and she has worked diligently to bring this dream to fruition. And for their gift of reading, many people will call her blessed.

We who have the privilege of knowing and loving her say:
Happy Birthday, Dear Lillian!
May God bless us with your presence for many birthdays yet to come.

Mother's Mirror
(An Essay)

I remember a spring day in April, a long time ago, when the yellow school bus stopped in front of our white frame house. My children—Carolyn, Chuck and Robyn—clattered down the bus steps, their faces bright, anticipating a few hours' play before dinner. Usually I was on the porch to greet them; but, today, hurrying to finish the ironing before Baby Verna awoke from her nap, I watched their arrival through the kitchen window.

Robyn was always last off the bus. It was her first year in school. She loved going. Her pixie face was all smiles, exposing a wide gap in her front teeth (the missing teeth went to the Tooth Fairy in exchange for a quarter). Between short plaid skirt and red knee socks, Robyn's short legs were winter pale in the spring sunshine. Descending the steps, she struggled to balance the heavy book satchel without falling into the shallow ditch bordering the unpaved road.

Carolyn and Chuck were already half-way up the driveway, yelling, "Mama, where are you?" They came bounding into the kitchen, not caring if they waked the sleeping baby, and dumped their books on the table. Giving me a quick hug, they hurried back outside to play with the dog, restricted to the clothesline because he chased cars. Knowing his release was imminent, Johnny greeted them with happy barks and wet licks. I watched through the window as they unhooked the leash, children and dog becoming an excited tangle on the cold ground.

This was the spring of 1962.
Winter in the northeast had been very cold, with much snow.

A military family (on orders of the Air Force), we had moved from Florida to Delaware the previous August. Having missed the Florida sunshine, we now waited impatiently for the return of spring. In the fall, my husband had planted dozens of Crocus bulbs. That morning, after the children had boarded the bus, I walked around the yard inspecting the bulbs in desperate search of a flower. In the protected ell of the house, I found a Crocus in bloom.

The yellow blossom brightened the gray morning—made my day. I could hardly wait until evening, when my husband came home, to share this eagerly awaited spring treasure. As I buttoned the final shirt on the clothes hanger, I wondered why Robyn hadn't come into the house. The door flew open. She came hurling into the kitchen, cheeks flushed and blond curls windblown. Dragging her book satchel by its strap, she cried excitedly, "I'm home, Mama, and guess what! I have a present for you!" One hand hidden behind her back, she gave me an angelic, toothless smile.

Before I saw ... I *knew*!

Releasing the book satchel, she danced forward, hugged me, and thrust out her small hand. In it was clutched my early spring—the yellow Crocus! Presenting the flower, she whispered softly, "I love you, Mama."

I wanted to forget that I was her loving mother and lash out, "Not my yellow Crocus, you naughty child!" I prayed silently, asked God's forgiveness for my anger. With tears in my eyes, I accepted Robyn's gift of love. Hugging her small body close, I felt my own heart expand with greater love. "Believe me, baby," I said softly, "I shall never forget this most precious gift."

Forty years later, the memory is still vivid.

Robyn is now the principal of a private school that teaches children who have dyslexia. Recently she wrote a poem, *Mother's Mirror*, and presented it to me. The Crocus (spring offering of love) is remembered. For in her reflections she writes, "You shine my childhood faces back to me. Will I disappear when you are gone?" My answer is no, dear daughter. With your kind and loving nature, and by God's grace, hopefully, you shall continue to bring joy to others as you have brought joy to me. May your life be filled with bright yellow Crocus … and may you continue to share them generously.

Mother's Mirror

Reflections:

me in your eyes
upside down
hanging from monkey bars
gravity overtaking curls

Reflections:

prized crocus
clasped in grubby hands
gap-toothed grin
spring offering

Reflections:

You shine my childhood
faces back at me.
Will I disappear
when you are gone?

—Robyn Rennick

Letter From Carolyn

Dearest Mom and Dad,

By the time you receive this, you will be grandparents. Congratulations!

I wished to take this special time to tell you I hope Howard and I do as well raising our babies as you did with us. I know there were times you wished you could have given us more materially than we had, but those things are far less important when paired with all the advantages we had. I hope Howard and I can share with our children the love you two shared with us in so many ways:

- the physical husband/wife love you were not embarrassed to display;
- the sacrificing of friends and home to move to a city that would enable us to get a better education without so much strain;
- the sense of family loyalty that enables us to fight with each other without becoming alienated and enables us to depend on each other;
- respect for our country;
- independence to stand for what we believe is right, even when everyone else is sitting;
- independence to make it on our own—to be proud to work;
- inner strength to know we can begin again should our world crumble;
- faith in God—His love and strength.

These examples are but a few of the things you have given us that I hope Howard and I are wise enough to give our babies.

I love you ...
Carolyn

Guilt

Tonight my bed is a straight jacket.
In mental anguish
I wrestle with an unwelcome bedfellow ...
Guilt.

For today I ignored the restraint of kindness, and
without compassion,
Maliciously attacked one who couldn't protect himself.
I'm ashamed!

Because of anger and resentment,
I refused to see beyond my injured feelings,
Criticizing and discouraging one already depressed;
And tonight I'm sleepless ...

I am being forced to look inside
Myself,
To delve into this quagmire of hypocrisy in
Search of compassion—for without compassion
There is no love.

Help me, O God, to love.

Praises

Praise you, O God, for your saving grace!
Praise you, O God, for accepting me!
Praise you for allowing me to call you Father!
Praise you for your compassion and love!
Praise you for hearing and answering when I pray!
Praise you for your healing touch!
Praise you for forgiving my transgressions!
Praise you for sending your Son,
Jesus,
That we may experience the depth of your love!
You are a great and merciful God, worthy of praise.
I shall praise and love You all the days of my life ...
And throughout eternity.

The Real Party Began

In my day:
The slumber party was a stay-over night
At the home of cousins,
Who were my best friends and neighbors.

Finished with supper—
And after the dishes were washed by us girls—
In the soft summer twilight
We gathered with the family on the front porch
To watch the firefly ballet in the meadow.

In winter months, we gathered in the kitchen
Around the cook stove.
There was corn-popping, sometimes candy-making,
And always storytelling.

We waited with dread
The striking of the grandfather clock in the hall;
For at nine o'clock the fun evening ended—
It was bedtime for this farm family.

We trouped upstairs, separated:
Parents to their bedroom, boys across the hall,
Girls climbing to the attic—being strongly cautioned to
"Blow out the kerosene lamp and go to sleep!"

In the bedroom under the eaves,
The large glass windows at either end
Spilling
Golden moonlight into the blue-black darkness,
The real party began!

Nestled in the warmth of the feather mattress,
We giggled, exchanged secrets, and discussed boys
Until sleep erased the present and
Filled our heads with dreams of the future—
Never to excel the happy memories of childhood.

Mother Is A Woman

Today has not been a good day.
Doubts fill my mind to overflowing, and
I'm suspicious of everyone;
For it appears everywhere I turn
I'm taken advantage of. ...

A woman on my own,
I have little working knowledge.
I'm at the mercy of the tradesman whom
I must deal with
Concerning repair and maintenance—
And I don't even speak his language!

I come away from those encounters
Seething,
Feeling that I have been taken advantage of!
Not because of my ignorance but
Because of my gender.

I'm not aggressive, feminist, nor anti-male;
I'm a pleasant and trusting woman—
Until victimized. ...
Then I become angry and defiant!

Are my suspicions warranted?
Does the tradesman deliberately exploit me
Because I am a female?
Has he forgotten that his
Mother is a woman?

A false balance is abomination to the Lord;
But a just weight is His delight. —Proverbs 1:11

Uniquely Woman

Self-esteem is born of a
Healthy psyche,
Nurtured by a spirit rich in self-love.
It isn't feminist,
Anti-male,
Nor an attitude.
Self-esteem is the right to be
Uniquely woman—
To develop the God-given attributes
That are uniquely mine.
Self-esteem promotes intellectual and
Spiritual growth,
Nurtures and enhances physical life.

And They Danced ...

And they danced and danced and danced ...
The surrounding walls disappearing into
Timeless, endless space.
They danced among the stars,
The spheres beating out a slow intoxicating rhythm. ...

And they danced and danced and danced ...
Escaping the gravity of planet,
Their bodies locked and swaying
Through a universe of star-clustered galaxies
In a dance mysterious. ...

And they danced and danced and danced ...
Entwined in harmony,
Moving in Rhythm,
Emotions fluid as the scale of the music. ...

And they danced and danced and danced. ...

Personal Epiphany

It is accepted by some scientists that
Our brain is genetically wired to respond to
Spiritual stimulation:
I knew that!
When I allow God entry into my life through
Prayer and meditation,
There is an intense surge of spiritual power;
I experience a personal epiphany—
The light of God's presence.

However, I'm in control of self.
When I forget to recharge my spiritual battery
Through religious practice,
The cells weaken and the light grows dim.
Overcome by fear of the impending darkness,
I cry out. ...
God who designed the circuitry of my brain immediately
Understands the problem and restores the connection.
Again
In the light of His presence, I'm safe.

A Season Continual

Created for a season,
We humans bud, bloom, and reach fruition,
Giving essence to a span of physical life;
Then we die.
But death isn't final, praise God!
Death is only transitional—
A passing from physical to spiritual life,
Where time is immeasurable;
Eternity is a season continual.

The Spirit of Praise

The opalescence of a new day:
Golden sunlight hallowing the landscape;
Birds proclaiming praise with melody;
Squirrels proclaiming praise with happy chatter.
A green lizard, expectantly awaiting breakfast,
Flicks its pink tongue in thanksgiving.
A mother watches the fast-disappearing school bus,
Gives praise for her beautiful child aboard.
In the fields, a farmer drives the tractor, turning
The rich, red soil,
Thanking God for its fertility.
God's presence and provision is everywhere.
Creator of all things, He provides for all creation.
Let us give thanks to Him for
Creating in each of us
The spirit of praise.

By Him were all things created that are in heaven,
And that are in earth. —Colossians !:16

I Am Satisfied

I pray much—
Mostly with my eyes wide open.
And while my prayers aren't always
Realistic or practical,
They are enriching, giving me
New perspectives and broader horizons—
A new realm in which to
Grow mentally and spiritually.

God listens.
He evaluates my prayers, and
Makes no mistakes;
Winnowing the chaff from the grain,
He provides the bread of life.
I am satisfied.

Your Father knoweth what things ye have need of
Before you ask him. —Matthew 6:8

It Takes Courage

It happens in mid-life,
After the hectic years of rearing children;
The nest is now empty.
Previously blind to anything not
Relating to family,
I am again in control of my life—
Have time to resume my
Career.
But it takes courage!
Courage to look into the mirror and
Acknowledge
That mature face as my own,
Bravely say, "Who cares,
I can do it!"
Then put on the "little" black dress,
Go out there—to the market place—and
"Wow 'em!"
Well, respectfully approach them—
These very young people who are in charge—
To humbly say, "Here am I,
Older, but capable and willing."

Cat

Cat has gone away and
I don't know where.
I have called, looked, hunted,
But all to no avail;
For he is not to be found.

Did someone entice him to
Follow them to another place?
I don't think so;
Cat and I were very compatible.
He was my best friend!

In the evening, when I went out,
Cat noticed,
But never complained.
He was patiently waiting on the driveway
When I returned,
His green eyes luminous.

As a faithful protector,
Cat accompanied me inside the house.
He walked through the rooms.
Satisfied that there were no intruders,
He went back outside to pursue his
Tomcat activities.

Cat has been gone for a year, but
I continue to look for him,
Miss him.
As a beloved friend,
He shall forever be remembered.

Life's Sunset

When we were children,
Life stretched to infinity;
When we became adults,
Infinity suddenly developed boundaries.
Now that we are old,
Infinity and boundaries merge into
A brief life span.

What is the secret to enjoying
Life's sunset years?
Is it to withdraw—become a recluse—
Spend our remaining days in
Self-gratification?

I think not!

Perhaps God is trying to get our
Attention!
Perhaps He is saying, "It is time to
Look outward,
Not inward—
To stop being in bondage to self,
See the needs of others,
Reach out …"

Reaching out, we lose our fear of
Approaching night;
The sunset is bright with opportunity.

Divine Fruit

Seeds planted in the garden of
Our Soul
In seasons of pain,
Watered by the storms of life,
Matured in the sunshine of
God's Grace,
Produce faith, love, joy, peace …
Divine Fruit.

Summertime In Maine

Granite mountains tall,
Lakes and crystalline waterfall,
Skies blue,
Sunshine bright,
Breeze fresh and exhilarating.
Purple lilacs and rosy-cheek apples,
Potatoes, rhubarb and blueberries,
Brown deer in quiet coves,
Moose hiding in green woods,
Red fox chasing ground-squirrel,
Bear cubs wrestling,
Loons screaming,
Fish jumping,
Black flies biting,
Lobster boiling in pots,
"Outsiders"
Overcrowding the rustic camps:
All together—
***Summertime In
Maine.***

Perfect Pitch

God's tuning fork—the dedicated Pastor,
Tuning
The human personality to harmonize
With the soul.

A spiritual melody in perfect pitch.

Proverb

An accepted proverb:
"Experience doesn't drip down."

Each of us makes our own mistakes,
And mistakes are countless.
Avoiding them—impossible!
Often we pray,
"God keep us from making mistakes."
In reality,
We should accept them as
Necessary tools of development,
Shaping productive lives.
While the shaping process is painful,
Learning is the hurt;
Growth is in the healing.

The Son of God

The Son of God
Came through natural childbirth so that
He would experience absolute humanness;
However, the spiritual man overshadowed
The physical man.

Jesus,
"Full of grace and truth,"
Was the total embodiment of God.
He invites you and me to *believe*,
With Him to become heirs of God.

The Holy Spirit shall come upon you,
And the power of God shall overshadow you;
So the baby from you will be utterly holy—
The Son of God. —Luke 55:56

Quick Fix

Busy people,
We think time is of the essence,
Seek a quick fix for our problems,
Tangible or intangible.

Tangible problems are easier to correct;
Intangible problems are the troublemakers.
They don't respond to the quick fix;
Need the help of a professional.

Intangible problems sometimes take
Years to work through;
We become so self-absorbed
We lose our perspective.

The answer to the problem eludes us.
Confused and hurting,
Finally
We release it to God.

Under His patient tutelage,
We better understand the problem; and,
Although it isn't solved, it is now acceptable.
He is the answer.

Hurricane

Hurricane-force winds blow.
Torrential rains pour.
Mud slides down the denuded mountains,
Crashing into the frenzied ocean, further incensing
Angry waves attacking eroding beaches.

It is a bleak, gray dawn:
The streets of Gonavies are strangely empty.
The masses of Haitian humanity
Fearfully huddle anyplace offering sanctuary from
Elements gone wild.

In a mean lean-to, the voodoo priests frantically
Pound their drums.
Sweat-lathered bodies sway to the throbbing tempo,
But they find no comfort in the music.
Their gods have forsaken them!

The hurricane intensifies:
Shacks are blown away, buildings collapse,
Houses disintegrate,
Floodwaters rush down the narrow streets—
A thousand Haitians die!

The voodoo drums are silent.

Birthday Surprise

I never see a violet blooming
In spring
That doesn't childish memories bring,
Of a sheltered bank under the hill—
The spring sunshine bright,
The March wind still.
A child on bent knee,
Picking every violet that
She could see.
For she must have a beautiful bouquet
(Of small-hand size)
For Mother's
Happy Birthday Surprise!

Focused

In a world of glitter and glamour,
My vision becomes severely distorted and
I miss the Righteous Path,
To become hopelessly lost in this
Labyrinth of worldliness. ...

The tentacles of the world tighten:
I desperately gaze heavenward—focus.
I see a single
Bright star—the guiding star—You, Lord!

Focused:
I struggle anew to escape impending doom;
But making no progress, I reach out—
You grasp my hand!
God's mysterious grace guiding me back into
The path of righteousness. ...

He will teach us His ways, and
We will walk in His paths. —Isaiah 2:3; Micah 4:2

Cultivate

In our lives,
God is the nurturing essence;
Life's yield reflects our commitment
To Him.
We can cultivate our faith or allow
It to lie fallow.
Cultivation
Produces a harvest that enriches and
Nourishes our souls.
If we choose not to cultivate,
Life becomes shallow.
Without roots our faith withers and dies.
So may the loam of our commitment
Be spiritually pulverized, that
The seeds of our faith are
Deeply rooted,
Producing an abundant crop of blessings.

Their souls shall be watered as a garden; and
They shall not sorrow any more at all. —Jeremiah 331:2

Life's Finished Tapestry

Mortal's years are but a weft in the
Warp of time.
Woven into the fabric of those years is
The accumulation of life:
Childhood, adulthood, marriage, parenthood
And advancing age,
Creating a unique design,
The person that we are becoming—and
Who is ofttimes a stranger.
For we continually experience change.
We are an unfinished work,
Not to be completed until the final
Rotation of the spindle.
We shall then see perfectly, without shadow,
Life's finished tapestry.
And may it be so pleasing that
We shall hear God whisper,
"A life well lived."

Invisible Dove

In a flood of trouble, we often forget God,
Send out our personal dove,
Thinking that it will find solid ground,
Return with an olive branch.

The flight proves fruitless;
The bird returns with an empty beak.
In frustration and anger
We denounce the dove.

Our faith weak,
We are now at the mercy of the storm.
The waters continue to rise;
We flounder helplessly and hopelessly.

As a last refuge
We look heavenward and cry out,
"Where are You, God?"
He hears our cry of distress. ...

The Spirit of God—invisible dove—
Descends and rests, calming the
Troubled waters.
Our faith revived, we find security
Under His wings.

In my distress I cried upon the Lord,
And he heard me. —Psalms 120:1

Never to Be Contained

Even before the creation,
God existed.
In Him was the Father;
The Holy Spirit;
The Son—
Three in One;
The all-encompassing
Trinity.
As there was no beginning with
God,
There is no end to
The scope of His infinite love.
He is the essence of
Life eternal—
Never to be contained.
His grace is free to all
Who in faith
Call upon His name.

For in Him dwelleth all the fullness
Of the Godhead bodily. —Colossians 2:9

Environmental Graveyard

The butterflies don't come any more.
I've planted some of their choice flowers—
Salvia, snapdragons, zinnias, and
My neighborhood is lush with milkweed ...
But all to no avail.

In past years, my butterfly garden was
Bright with the jeweled, winged Epicureans,
Especially the Monarch.
But no more. ... Where have they gone?

Will my grandchildren never
Experience the beauty of the butterfly
As I have known it?
Never experience the joy of seeing the
Colorful Lepidoptera
Delicately sipping flower nectar?

God looks down upon Earth and
Sadly shakes his head.
For man—and butterflies—He created
The perfect garden.
Is it destined to become an
Environmental graveyard?

He hath established it,
He created it not in vain,
He formed it to be inhabited. —Isaiah 45:18

Blaze A Trail

My small granddaughter asked,
"Grandma,
Which way does the earth turn?"
I punctually replied,
"It revolves counterclockwise,
Right around the sun."

Then, after some deep thought,
I wished it were true,
That the Earth did revolve
Right around the Son—God's Son,
The Light of the Universe;

That when we tell our children to
"Walk right,"
We don't walk in the opposite direction,
Confusing them.

For to follow God's Son
Is to walk right in His footsteps,
To blaze a trail—a trail of
Unmistakable Sonlight—
So our little ones may follow.

The Son of Man has come
To save that which is lost. —Matthew 18:11

For A Moment

Lord, I don't know how much
Time you will give me.
And it matters little at all;
It is best to love great
For a moment,
Than to forever love only small.

Although youth has departed my body—
The sinews and muscles are weak,
My heart ignores the change;
My emotions course true and deep.

I had begun to believe it was
Finished—
Life as I had known it before—
Then, this throbbing and exciting emotion
Came beating at heart's door.

Please forgive me if I'm foolish,
Act again the silly girl.
It is exhilarating to be in love;
It lights up the evening of my world.

Presence of the Moment

Never having learned to live in
The completeness of
Life now,
We mentally invade the future—
Living events before they occur.

When the future becomes the
Present,
The excitement is gone;
The event has become insipid.
It has been savored to death.
For satisfaction is found only in the
Presence of the moment.

The Open Door

Jesus was betrayed with a kiss,
Denied with an oath,
Falsely accused,
Scourged and delivered to be crucified.
Wearing a crown of platted thorns,
He was nailed to a cross,
Ridiculed by all who passed by.

In the sixth hour
The earth in horror and shame convulsed,
Covering its sorrow in darkness.
In the ninth hour with a loud cry,
Jesus dismissed his spirit.

Dawn of the third day,
Streams of celestial light flooded
The garden of the sepulcher where
Jesus was buried,
Found entrance to the tomb through
The open door,
Invading its darkness,
Exposing its emptiness.

Jesus' resurrection:
His victory over death and the grave.
For His children:
A valid passport to Eternal Life.
Hallelujah! Amen!

Eternal Fellowship

Pilate said:
"I find no fault in this man.
I will chastise him and release him."
The people screamed, "Crucify him! Crucify him!"

Jesus was crucified—not for what he did:
Healing the sick,
Restoring sight to the blind,
Showing compassion for the poor,
Raising the dead—
But for who He was and why He came.

The Son of God.
He came to make atonement for man's sin
By dying on the cross.
The third day, Jesus rose from the dead.
After appearing to his disciples,
He ascended into Heaven.

Through the grace of His sacrificial love
(Easter and forevermore),
We are redeemed and assured of
Eternal life with Him.

A Red Traffic Light

I sat in my car waiting for the
Red traffic light to change to green.
Looking down the broad thoroughfare at the
Slow-moving caravan of homeward-bound vehicles,
Their headlights disks of blinding brightness in
The early dusk of the winter evening,
I envisioned:
Inside the man-made bodies of steel,
Secured by man-made safety belts,
A microcosm of the world's people,
Experiencing
The ongoing complexities of life:
Joy, sorrow, hope, fear, health, ill health,
Tears and laughter. ...
A red traffic light—
A moment of contemplation ...
A prayer of intercession.

Twilight

My life is being lived in the
Twilight;
Everywhere I turn there is sadness.
My peers are "passing on" and
I can't seem to adjust.
The world I previously enjoyed is
In shadow—empty and isolated.
A world in which
I'm no longer a participant.

In a state of depression, I wait ...
Wait for what? I *know*,
And I hate this premonition.
I want my former jubilance back!
The happy anticipation that
Tomorrow's sunshine will eliminate
Today's dark shadow.
Tears will be but residue of
Happy laughter.
Then, I shall again enjoy living.

Hawaiian Paradise

God looked down upon the earth,
Seeing a great expanse of water reflecting
The blue of the sky.
It was a lovely, but lonely, sight;
For in the vast waters there was nothing
On which to rest the eyes.
The great ocean needed substance.
He nodded and smiled. ...

Gazing deep into the water,
God saw steam rising from fissures,
Releasing the heat from Earth's interior.
He waved his hand over the water and
Caldrons burst forth,
Exploding geysers of boiling black lava.
God's attention was momentarily diverted. ...

He returned to the
Exciting, happy, happenings in paradise.
And, as you know,
A moment with God (measured in Earth time),
Could be a thousand years. ...
When He again focused on those waters,
Something unusual had occurred:
Protruding from the ocean waves were
Barren, conical-shaped mountains, some
Continuing to erupt fiery lava.
The Hawaiian Islands were thus born!

Islands:
Extending across the azure water for
More than a thousand miles. ...
God gleefully clapped his hands;

Rain poured down upon the islands, creating
Laughing waterfalls and dancing streams.
God again returned to Paradise.
A millennium later, He revisited Earth. ...
The chain of islands, formerly barren,
Were now a lush and vibrant green.

God blessed the islands with
Fruit-bearing trees,
Gardens of exotic flowers,
Song birds with colorful plumage. ...
In a playful mood,
He pointed toward the ocean.
A pair of white whales surfaced—spouting.
He laughed aloud. ...
Everything God had made was very good!
On Planet Earth
He had created a Hawaiian Paradise.

Messenger Of Grace

I woke with depression,
Sought God in prayer,
But my mind was so tormented,
I did not find Him there.

Then, just outside my window,
A bird began to sing.
As I listened,
My depression took wing.

The joy in its song
Brought a smile to my face.
I knew that the bird was
His messenger of grace.

"Free as a bird,"
Is an adage of old;
And if we listen with faith,
God will make us as bold.

If you suffer depression,
Don't yield to despair;
Open the windows of your soul ...
There's a song out there!

The Star

In the dusk of early evening
The lights of Bethlehem were welcome beacons to
The weary travelers.
Leading the donkey, the man lengthened his stride.
On the donkey's back, the woman who was large with child
Whispered a prayer of thanksgiving.

Outside for a breath of evening air,
The innkeeper watched their approach.
He shook his head before the man could speak,
"There is no room in the inn."
Seeing the woman's condition, his heart was
Strangely touched.
He pointed toward the cave in the hillside,
"The stable—
It is warm, and there is plenty of clean straw. ..."
The man looked at the woman. She nodded assent.

The innkeeper was surprised to hear himself saying,
"I'll send thee my wife, she is good at birthing."
The woman said, "Hurry, please ..."
As the travelers disappeared into the stable,
The innkeeper noticed the star. It was
The largest and brightest star that he had ever seen.
It hung directly over the stable.

Unafraid

From the cauldrons of evil
Boil the horrors of WAR;
But I am unafraid.
My faith is securely anchored in
Jesus,
The Cross and Open Tomb.
Eternal is His sovereignty;
Absolute is His power.
Protected by His divine grace,
Secure in His unchangeable love,
I am unafraid.

Paula's Spirit

I have thought of her so much, Paula. ...
She was beautiful, outward and inward.
She had dancing dark eyes, curly black hair, and
Dimples flashed provocatively when she smiled
(which was often),
And a heart that was kind and loving.

She was seventeen—a senior in high school,
And very popular.
It appeared that she was particularly blessed;
The world was hers for the taking;
Then it happened ...

Paula's energy level dropped and
Her sleep pattern changed; she
Had no appetite for fast food—or any food.
Her eyes lost their sparkle—fear now lurked there.
The family doctor and other doctors ran many tests,
Compared notes, and made the diagnosis ...

Paula had leukemia—the worst kind!
The family was devastated but
Paula kept her faith.
She assured her family and friends
That she would beat the leukemia—get well.

She tried—how hard she tried!
But life as Paula had previously known it was past.
Her life now revolved around visits to the doctor's office.
Then came hospitalization and transfusions.
For a while she'd regain strength—but the
Leukemia was relentless. ...
Her body became frail—tired beyond endurance. ...

Doctors, family, friends, did their best;
No one wanted to lose this beautiful, brave girl,
But time ran out.
Again in the hospital, pale and wan, Paula whispered,
"Daddy, I want to go home."
Gathering the frail body into his arms, he whispered,
"Soon, baby, I'll take you home soon."

Paula smiled, snuggled deeper into his arms,
And drifted off to sleep.
He gently tucked her back into bed,
Resumed his anxious watch.

Soon thereafter, with a sigh, a smile—
An expression of peace on her angelic face,
Paula's journey was finished.
Escaping the pain of the physical body,
Paula went home;
Her spirit soaring joyfully to meet God.

PAN

PAN went away today:
Where he went, well, I'm not quite sure,
But I'm guessing that God has a
Special place for deceased pets that
Have brought so much happiness into our lives.
I would hope, upon leaving this world,
God gathers the love exuded by
Our beloved pets,
Compresses it into an energizing force
To be distributed to lonely people without pets—
Renewing and enriching their lives.
That is what PAN's love did for me.
Thank you, PAN.
I shall never forget your unconditional Love.
Rest in peace. ...

Sweetening the Filling

Frustration—frustration—frustration—
Every way I turn is frustration!
I burn the pie filling, ruin my best kettle,
Boil the tea to a black draught,
Burn my hand, break the tea pitcher.
Then I lose it!
My husband tries to console me but
I refuse to be consoled.
Running outside, I sit on the bench among
The day lilies.
Looking up into the serenely blue sky,
Silently cry, "Help me, Father!"

After a time of contemplation,
God gently quiets my angry frustration.
Now contrite,
I pick a handful of brightly colored day lilies,
A peace offering for my husband, who forgives
My bad humor.
He tenderly kisses my burned hand.
I make another pie—
God's grace and my husband's love
Sweetening the filling.

Family Reunion

The generation of women present preceded
Women's lib,
Plastic surgery, Botox, and popular low-carb diets.
Their spa activity: chasing kids, cleaning house,
And tending the vegetable garden;
Their pleasantly plump bodies sculpted by good living.
Their life's challenge:
Making a home, rearing a family, being a good neighbor;
Their mature, serenely beautiful faces reflecting
This Godly commitment.

Silver-haired men, eyes clear and appraising,
Extend work-rough hands,
The persona of strength, character, faith.
These men,
The foundation on which family and country
Rested securely—
A generation to be forever remembered as
"The Greatest Generation."

A family reunion:
Families sharing past memories, present joys,
Pictures of grandchildren;
Their golden dreams for the future …

Cancer

CANCER—the diagnosis we dread to hear;
Has the resounding ring of doom upon my reluctant ear:
That moment my life becomes the Titanic;
I begin to drown in fear.
The shoreline recedes;
I clutch at waves of happy memories;
Try to keep my head about the devastating tide.
The current is strong;
Obliterating past memories and future dreams.
I am going down for the third time. ...
I cry out, "Please, God, I don't want to die!"
Then deep inside—beneath the drowning fear,
A tide of warmth rises;
My soul has buoyancy!
The icy waters of panic subside.
I hear a quiet voice:
"For God hath not given us the spirit of fear; but of power, and
Of love, and a sound mind."
My head rises above the turbulent water;
I draw a deep breath of pure air, slowly exhale ...
My faith is restored.
I trust God's love and power to help me overcome the
Fear of cancer—through Him, whatever the final result,
I shall keep a sound mind.

Birthdays

Birthdays aren't to be measured in years,
Rather
In happiness, laughter, and ofttimes tears.
Years to be welcomed as the seasons:
Winter, spring, summer, fall;
Then we wouldn't mind the years at all.
We would give thanks to God for
Longevity and maturity, trusting Him for
Eternal security.

Birthday—Again

It's my birthday—again—
And so many have already been.
I look back through the years, remembering
Seasons of sunshine and tears—
Both needed for growth.
I look at myself in the mirror and
I have grown ... older ...
There are lines in my face;
My hair is all streaked with white;
And my body isn't what it used to be.
But I smile; for, to me,
I'm a beautiful sight—I'm alive!
And for all the years that have been—
And those yet to be—
Thanks be to God!

Glory of Christmas

The house was aglow with Christmas lights;
The tree beautifully decorated;
The gifts under it wrapped in gold paper and
Tied with red ribbons.
Aroma of baking turkey assailed the nostrils,
Tantalizing the taste buds.
But something was wrong—something was
Missing!
Reviewing the list of holiday preparations,
I decided all had been completed.
Then, it became heartbreakingly apparent:
In the hustle-bustle of festivity,
Jesus,
Whom we were honoring, had been forgotten.
He was not invited to attend His own
Birthday celebration!
Sinking to my knees, I urgently prayed,
"Forgive me, Jesus!
Forgetting You, the Spirit of Christmas is lost."
I invited Him back into my life, that
The miracle of His birth
Might brighten all my days with the
GLORY OF CHRISTMAS.

Promise of Peace

In a world where we cry peace,
But there is no peace,
We reflect upon the Babe of Bethlehem,
God's gift of love and peace.
Revisiting the manger scene again and again,
The refrain of angels' singing
"Peace on earth; good will to men"
Restores our faith.
We believe all things are possible
Through Christ Jesus.

Prayer Is the Formula

Tormented within and without,
I shake my fist heavenward, angrily shout,
"Why me, God?"
What have I done? I'm so unhappy—
Having no fun!

My seizure of self-pity spent,
I look around and see
The blessings that He's sent:
A world of beauty, sunshine and fresh air—
Inhabited by "loved ones" who care.

Blinders removed—ashamed and contrite,
I recover my sight.
Oh, the troubles remain,
But now I address them
In His loving name.

He always hears my prayer—
Helps me with my burdens of care.
So when self-pity holds me sway,
Prayer is the formula to
Chase it away.

About the Author

Jackie Rennick is a Virginian by birth but has called Florida home for many years. As the wife of a military man, she was privileged to travel the world. Living in many places, she developed a variety of interests, which are reflected in her poetry. She has been published in *Celebration of Poets, Best Poems of 1998, Outstanding Poets of 1998, America at the Millennium, The Best Poems and Poets of 2001, Essence of a Dream, Decision Magazine,* and other publications. Jackie has received four Editor's Awards. In the year 2000, she was awarded a Certificate of Merit by Writer's Digest Books for her book of poetry, *A Glimpse of the Soul.* She also is the author of *When Morning Comes,* a novel (2004).

Jackie is the mother of five grown children—Carolyn, Chuck, Robyn, Verna, and adopted daughter Patricia. She is active in church and civic organizations and enjoys fishing, reading and travel. She recently visited the Hawaiian Islands. Her greatest thrill was a trip to China and walking on the Great Wall. She also has lived in Japan. When her grandchildren are seniors in high school, she takes them to visit a country of their choice. They have traveled to Italy, France and England.

A widow for many years, Jackie recently married Dr. Thomas R. King, professor emeritus, Department of Communications, Florida State University. They live in Tallahassee, Florida.

Graphics by Kent E. King, a graduate of Savannah College of Art & Design.